J E

M000113838

Jesus

PROVOCATIVE TEACHER

BILL DONAHUE

IVP Connect

InterVarsity Press
Downers Grove, Illinois

Inter-Varsity Press
Leicester, England

InterVarsity Press, USA
P.O. Box 1400, Downers Grove, IL 60515-1426, USA
World Wide Web: www.ivpress.com
E-mail: email@ivpress.com

Inter-Varsity Press, England
Norton Street, Nottingham NG7 3HR, England
Website: www.ivpbooks.com
E-mail: ivp@ivpbooks.com

InterVarsity Press®, USA, is the book-publishing division of InterVarsity Christian Fellowship/USA®, a student movement active on campus at hundreds of universities, colleges and schools of nursing in the United States of America, and a member movement of the International Fellowship of Evangelical Students. For information about local and regional activities, write Public Relations Dept., InterVarsity Christian Fellowship/USA, 6400 Schroeder Rd., P.O. Box 7895, Madison, WI 53707-7895, or visit the IVCF website at <www.intervarsity.org>.

Inter-Varsity Press, England, is closely linked with the Universities and Colleges Christian Fellowship (formerly the Inter-Varsity Fellowship), a student movement linking Christian Unions in universities and colleges throughout Great Britain, and a member movement of the International Fellowship of Evangelical Students. For information about local and national activities write to UCCF, 38 De Montfort Street, Leicester LE1 7GP, email them at email@uccf.org.uk, or visit the UCCF website at www.uccf.org.uk.

Design: Cindy Kiple
Images: Seide Preis/Getty Images

USA ISBN 978-0-8308-2151-8

UK ISBN 978-1-84474-115-1

Printed in the United States of America ∞

| P | 20 | 19 | 18 | 17 | 16 | 15 | 14 | 13 | 12 | 11 | 10 | 9 | 8 | 7 | 6 | 5 | 4 | 3 | 2 |
| Y | 23 | 22 | 21 | 20 | 19 | 18 | 17 | 16 | 15 | 14 | 13 | 12 | 11 | | 10 | 09 | 08 | 07 | |

CONTENTS

BEFORE YOU BEGIN

The Jesus 101 series is designed to help you respond to Jesus as you encounter him in the stories and teachings of the Bible, particularly the Gospel accounts of the New Testament. The "101" designation does not mean "simple"; it means "initial." You probably took introductory-level courses in high school or at a university, like Economics 101 or Biology 101. Each was an initial course, a first encounter with the teachings and principles of the subject matter. I had my first encounter with economic theory in Econ 101, but it was not necessarily simple or always easy (at least not for me!).

Jesus 101 may be the first time you looked closely at Jesus. For the first time you will encounter his grace and love, be exposed to his passion and mission, and get a firsthand look at the way he connects with people like you and me. Or perhaps, like me, you have been a Christian many years. In that case you will encounter Jesus for the first time all over again. Often when I read a biblical account of an event in Jesus' life, even if the text is very familiar to me, I am amazed at a new insight or a fresh, personal connection with Jesus I hadn't experienced before.

I believe Jesus 101 will challenge your thinking and stir your soul regardless of how far along the spiritual pathway you might be. After all, Jesus is anything but dull: he tended to shake up the world of everyone who interacted with him. Sometimes people sought him out; often he surprised them. In every case, he challenged them, evoking a reaction they could hardly ignore.

There are many ways we might encounter Jesus. In this series we will focus on eight. You will come face to face with Jesus as

- Provocative Teacher
- Sacred Friend
- Extreme Forgiver
- Authentic Leader
- Truthful Revealer
- Compassionate Healer
- Relentless Lover
- Supreme Conqueror

☐ How These Guides Are Put Together

In each of the discussion guides you will find material for six group meetings, though feel free to use as many meetings as necessary to cover the material. That is up to you. Each group will find its way. The important thing is to encounter and connect with Christ, listen to what he is saying, watch what he is doing—and then personalize that encounter individually and as a group.

The material is designed to help you engage with one another, with the Bible and with the person of Jesus. The experiences below are designed to guide you along when you come together as a group.

Gathering to Listen

This short section orients you to the material by using an illustration, a quote or a text that raises probing questions, makes provocative assumptions or statements, or evokes interpersonal tension or thoughtfulness. It may just make you laugh. It sets the tone for the dialogue you will be having together. Take a moment here to connect with one another and focus your attention on the reading. Listen carefully as thoughts and emotions are stirred.

After the reading, you will have an opportunity to respond in some way. What are your first impressions, your assumptions, disagreements, feelings? What comes to mind as you read this?

Encountering Jesus

Here you meet Jesus as he is described in the Bible text. You will encounter his teachings, his personal style and his encounters with people much like you. This section will invite your observations, questions and initial reactions to what Jesus is saying and doing.

Joining the Conversation

A series of group questions and interactions will encourage your little community to engage with one another about the person and story of Jesus. Here you will remain for a few moments in the company of Jesus and of one another. This section may pose a question about your group or ask you to engage in an exercise or interaction with one another. The goal is to discover a sense of community as you question and discover what God is doing.

Connecting Our Stories

Here you are invited to connect your story (life, issues, questions, challenges) with Jesus' story (his teaching, character and actions). We look at our background and history, the things that encourage or disappoint us. We seek to discover what God is doing in our life and the lives of others, and we develop a sense of belonging and understanding.

Finding Our Way

A final section of comments and questions invites you to investigate next steps for your spiritual journey as a group and personally. It will evoke and prompt further action, decisions or conversations in response to what was discovered and discussed. You will prompt one another to listen to God more deeply, take relational risks and invite God's work in your group and in the community around you.

Praying Together

God's Holy Spirit is eager to teach you! Remember that learning is not just a mental activity; it involves relationship and action. One educator suggests that all learning is the result of failed expectations. We hope, then, that at some point your own expectations will fail, that you will be ambushed by the truth and stumble into new and unfamiliar territory that startles you into new ways of thinking about God and relating to him through Christ. And so prayer—talking and listening to God—is a vital part of the Jesus 101 journey.

If you are seeking to discover Jesus for the first time, your prayer can be a very simple expression of your thoughts and questions to God. It may include emotions like anger, frustration, joy or wonder. If you already have an intimate, conversational relationship with God, your prayer will reflect the deepest longings and desires of your soul. Prayer is an integral part of the spiritual life, and small groups are a great place to explore it.

Consider This

In this section you'll find some ideas of ways to continue thinking and learning about the topics of the study. Pick one of these to work on during the week.

☐ HOW DO I PREPARE?

No preparation is required! Reading the Bible text ahead of time, if you can, will provide an overview of what lies ahead and will give you an opportunity to reflect on the Bible passages. But you will not feel out of the loop or penalized in some way if you do not get to it. This material is designed for *group* discovery and interaction. A sense of team and community develops and excitement grows as you explore the material together. In contrast to merely discussing what everyone has already discovered prior to the meeting, "discovery in the moment" evokes a sense of shared adventure.

If you want homework, do that after each session. Decide how you might face your week, your job, your relationships and family in light of what you have just discovered about Jesus.

☐ A FINAL NOTE

These studies are based on the book *In the Company of Jesus*. It is not required that you read the book to do any Jesus 101 study—each stands alone. But you might consider reading the parallel sections of the book to enrich your experience between small group meetings. The major sections of the book take up the same eight ways that we encounter Jesus in the Jesus 101 guides. So the eight guides mirror the book in structure and themes, but the material in the book is not identical to that of the guides.

Jesus 101 probes more deeply into the subject matter, whereas *In the Company of Jesus* is designed for devotional and contemplative reading and prayer. It is filled with stories and anecdotes to inspire and motivate you in your relationship with Christ.

I pray and hope that you enjoy this adventure as you draw truth from the Word of God for personal transformation, group growth and living out God's purposes in the world!

INTRODUCTION

THE PROVOCATIVE TEACHER

Jesus of Nazareth was no bore. No one ever left a session with Jesus and said "Oh well, that was interesting. Hey, did anyone see Myron's new camel?" Not after Jesus finished talking.

His teaching was anything but conventional.

Unsettling? Often.

Irritating? On occasion.

Boring? Never.

Provocative? Always.

Provocative. This English word has it roots in the Latin *provocare,* which means "to call forth." Yes, Jesus *provokes* people.

Jesus' words elicit stunned silence one moment and a near insurrection the next. At times he even seems contradictory or simply befuddling. "I came that you might have life, and have it to the full." *Yes, Jesus, now you're talkin'!* "So come, die with me, deny yourself, and pick up your cross every day." *Did I miss something here? Is this his idea of life to the fullest? Communal capital punishment?*

Casual observers, caustic critics and committed followers alike were caught off guard by such pronouncements. Is this Jesus of Nazareth schizophrenic? Is he confused? Is it time for us to begin waving and chanting, "Flip-flop, flip-flop!" Let's face it: this is poor image management, to say the least. Perhaps Jesus needs a political consultant to keep him on message and to develop a stump talk that will promise everything and offend no one, with enough sound bites for quippy TV ads.

But Jesus didn't come to capture votes—he came to liberate hearts. His teaching was designed to confront women and men with the realities and hopes of life in an ongoing relationship with God, not the temporal realm of this world's systems. To move us from our world toward his, he often prods us with startling assertions and soul-searching questions. He is the great Unsettler.

Jesus' teaching was true grit, illustrated with everyday objects like mustard seeds and stones, water and sand, even once using a child as a prop. He used word pictures as he told his stories, lacing his parables with pungent truth and uncommon wisdom.

Open your mind and heart to an encounter with Jesus, the Provocative Teacher. Come near and listen. And prepare for some wonderfully unsettling moments.

ONE

Jesus

SHATTERS OUR ILLUSIONS

You have heard that it was said . . . but I say . . .

☐ GATHERING TO LISTEN

About a month before graduating from college, I was looking at apartments in New York City, where I expected to work in June 1980. After finding one that fit my budget, I asked the manager if she could hold the apartment until I confirmed with my boss the actual date I would be moving in. "Sure," she said. "But I need a $50 deposit to hold it."

"But what if things change and I can't move in?" I asked.

"No problem. Just call me and I'll return the deposit."

Two weeks later, my new boss realigned the sales territories for our division, and I needed to look elsewhere for living arrangements. So I contacted the manager and asked her to refund the money. "I can't do that," she said.

"But that was our deal," I argued.

"The deposit is nonrefundable. It is too late to return it at this point." She hung up the phone and never returned further calls. I had no time or legal resources to pursue the matter further. Anyway, $50 was too little money to justify any legal action. And she knew it.

I had been under the illusion that a deal was a deal, that when people signed papers and set contracts it meant that there was a commitment. There was trust. I had seen stories of fraud on the evening news, but I had never been swindled myself. Now I knew. This world—at least the world I was entering—was different from the one I had envisioned. It was a world where professionals cheated and lied, where a handshake meant nothing and a deal was only as good as the lawyers you had standing behind it. I had gotten my wake-up call.

- Describe a time you felt disillusioned, let down or disappointed. Why was this experience so unnerving? What "illusions" were you operating under?

☐ ENCOUNTERING JESUS

No one likes to feel disillusioned. It is a downer. Dreams are shattered, expectations go unmet. The awareness of loss or abandonment can lurk in the recesses of our hearts and minds for days or weeks. Disappointment is, well, disappointing. Yet in some cases disillusionment may actually open us up to the ways of Jesus and our understanding of God.

To be dis-illusioned is to have our illusions "dissed," removed or shattered. Suddenly, sometimes dramatically and often unexpectedly, we are forced to abandon one picture of reality for another. If we have been operating under a false reality, it is actually good to have those illusions removed—*dissed*—so that we can embrace a new reality, a true reality.

Read Matthew 5:1-12.

1. These verses are called "the Beatitudes," and they describe the qualities of those who are *blessed*. What strikes you most as you read these beatitudes?

The kingdom of God is a Bible term used to describe the rule and reign of God in the world. It is a life-giving rule, not an oppressive form of tyranny.

2. How would Jesus' statements disturb people in the crowd and be provocative? Consider especially the following groups that may have been represented there—what might they be thinking?

   - Pharisees and other religious leaders
   - widows and orphans
   - Jesus' closest followers
   - a Roman centurion
   - a single mother
   - a slave working on the land of a vineyard owner
   - Roman politicians

The Pharisees represented a ruling sect of Jewish religious leaders. They were considered to be experts in the Old Testament laws but were known to be quite strict and legalistic.

A centurion commanded a hundred Roman soldiers. They were the most popular of Roman military personnel seen in the Palestinian region.

☐ JOINING THE CONVERSATION

3. We all have a way we view the world—some call this a "worldview" or "frame of reference" through which we observe life and make judgments. Using the list below to prompt your thinking, respond to the question, *What most influences my view of the world?* There may be several factors or just one.

   • my political orientation
   • my religious views
   • my assumptions about what ought to be true
   • the opinions of friends or family
   • authority figures I trust
   • the Bible or another text

4. In what ways do these influences affect your ability to see truth?

☐ CONNECTING OUR STORIES

5. Look again at the statements in Matthew 5:3-12 and complete the following sentences.

   I was glad when Jesus said, "Blessed are _____ "
   because . . . _____.

   I was uncomfortable when Jesus said, "Blessed are _____
   _____ " because . . . _____.

6. When we read some of Jesus' statements, like "Blessed are the merciful," we might say to ourselves, *Yes—that's the way it ought to be!* But what do we do with a Jesus who also enthusiastically blesses those who are insulted and persecuted, in verses 10-12? Do you dismiss his words? If not, what do you make of such statements?

7. How have your upbringing and previous religious experiences influenced the way you respond to Jesus' words?

☐ FINDING OUR WAY

8. Jesus' words always elicit a response. These first few verses in his message shatter the illusions of listeners and set the tone for what follows—the Sermon on the Mount recorded in Matthew 5—7. How do these words "provoke" you? (Do they bring hope? create more questions? arouse deep thoughts? inspire change? do you feel "blessed" as you read these words?)

9. Here's the risk. Having our illusions shattered is initially painful and disconcerting, maybe even humiliating. But it may also free us to participate in a whole new world of experiences with the God and his people. What will it take for you to embark on such an adventure into the unknown?

☐ PRAYING TOGETHER

Take some time to examine your illusions about Jesus and his approach to life. Ask God to open your eyes to his truth. Pray for courage to face the unknown and to experience the uncomfortable, in order that you might encounter God's power at work in your life and in the world around you. Consider praying through these blessing statements by personalizing them. For example, "Dear God, I know we will receive your blessing when we recognize our poverty of spirit and seek the countercultural life you are offering."

☐ CONSIDER THIS

Here are some ways for you to continue thinking about the topics of this session. Choose one to pursue this week.

- Pick one of the beatitudes and meditate on it each day of the week, and review your day in the evening. Ask the Holy Spirit to reveal areas of growth that day as you tried to be more aware of Jesus' countercultural life orientation.

- Begin to write out some thoughts about your illusions. How has Jesus confronted them? What needs to change about them? Are some valid? Are you holding on to some because you are afraid of the new reality?

- Put Jesus' teaching to the test. List people who exhibit meekness or poverty of spirit or who are merciful, for example. Observe their lives—are they truly "blessed"?

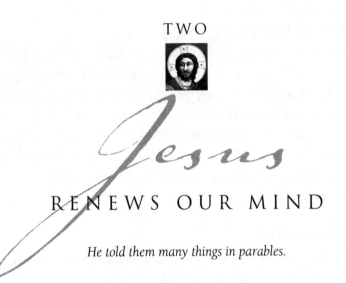

TWO

Jesus RENEWS OUR MIND

He told them many things in parables.

GATHERING TO LISTEN

I feel as though David Bradley has saved my life—at least my work life—
dozens of times, and I'd thank him if he were still with us. Bradley, who
retired from IBM in 2004, invented the Control-Alt-Delete sequence that
saves our computers from crashing when the system locks up and our
entire life (well, a lot of its data) is about to vaporize before our eyes.

Long before that safeguard was commonplace, my PC went into a
nosedive with a thirty-page Greek exegesis paper on the screen. An exe-
getical paper requires dozens of hours of research in the Greek text of
the New Testament, so it is a lot like any research assignment, except for
that especially fun Greek aspect. Late in the evening before the paper
was due, I was working feverishly and had not backed up my writing in
many hours. Then the system locked up, and the paper was gone—forever. With Control-Alt-Delete I could have retrieved at least a large portion of it. As it was, I had to resort to the "my computer wiped it out"
excuse when I faced my professor.

It would be great if we could reboot our *mind* now and then, don't you think? But we are more than a mere conglomeration of circuits, motherboards and disk drives, and God didn't wire a Refresh button or a spiritual version of Control-Alt-Delete into our human frame. We actually have something better, though—not quicker or faster, but more transforming. We need more than a reset: we need change and growth. We need Christ's work inside us if we are to understand the ways of Jesus.

"Be transformed by the renewing of your mind," wrote Paul to the Romans (12:2). Not mind replacement. Not mind control. Not an emptying of the mind, as Eastern mystics teach. No, we need mind *renewal*—an ongoing process working in us. A fresh start, a crisp outlook, a new way of thinking that improves with maturity in faith. But we cannot do it alone; someone has to do the cleanup. That someone is Jesus.

- Take some time and reflect back on a "fresh start" moment in your life. It may have been a new position or assignment at work, recovery from a painful divorce, coming home after an illness or a trip to the emergency room, or the birth of a child. How did this experience change you?

☐ ENCOUNTERING JESUS

In this passage Jesus tells a parable. A parable is a story that uses everyday objects or situations to communicate a deeper spiritual truth. Jesus used such stories to draw the openhearted and to befuddle those who had hardened their hearts to him and to God's truth. Parables usually have one central theme and use metaphors to convey that theme.

Read Matthew 13:1-9.

1. Before looking more deeply at the teaching in this story, make a few observations about Jesus, the provocative teacher. What strikes you about his approach?

How does he connect with the audience?

2. In verse 9 Jesus says, "He who has ears, let him hear." Now there may be a few in the crowd who have hearing disabilities, but everyone else is listening with functional ears. What might Jesus be trying to say here?

So far so good: Jesus is telling a nice story. But then his closest followers ask him why he speaks in parables. **Read Matthew 13:10-23.**

3. Is Jesus just saying, "The rich get richer and the poor get poorer" in verses 11-12? How do you respond to this statement?

4. What about verse 15? It might seem that Jesus is saying, "I speak to them in parables so that they will not understand what I am saying. If they did understand, they might get healed, and we sure don't want that to happen." What is Jesus getting at?

☐ **JOINING THE CONVERSATION**

5. Based on verse 15, why is it dangerous to block out the truth and harden yourself against it?

The Bible uses heart and mind almost interchange-ably at times, reflecting the Hebrew view of a person as holistic and interconnected. This is in contrast to a Western, Greco-Roman approach in which categories are more distinct and separate.

6. Jesus is dropping clues for seekers of truth, especially in verses 15 and 19. He wants listeners to think differently about spiritual growth and how we receive truth. So he tells parables to enlighten people about the mysteries of the kingdom. How would you rate the elastic-ity of your heart? Why?

   • soft and pliable • a little crusty • harder than I'd like to admit

7. Which of the options below do you think others might choose to de-scribe you? Circle all that apply.

   • very open to new ideas
   • thinks deeply about ideas and opinions
   • a little close-minded
   • has firm convictions and beliefs
   • strongly defends opinions and beliefs
   • has to be right all the time
   • stubborn and bull-headed
   • undecided

   What does this reveal about you?

OLD TESTAMENT INSIGHT

Jesus quotes Isaiah 6:9-10, a message of judgment for the Israelite people for their unfaithfulness to their loving God. The Israelites had repeatedly rejected God's messengers and his message, shunning his love, protection and help. Instead of repenting when prophets brought truth, they worshiped idols instead of God.

Opportunities to hear the truth do not always change people's hearts in positive ways. In some cases hearing the truth has a hardening effect.

☐ **CONNECTING OUR STORIES**

8. What would your small group community look like a year from now if people's hearts become increasingly open to the ways and teachings of Jesus?

Conversely, what might the group be like if hearts get harder and minds get cynical?

How do we guard against this?

9. Truth seekers find that they hunger for the living Word of God, even though they know it might challenge them, make them feel ashamed or prod them toward major changes. Where are you in this regard? Have you hardened your heart to the truth in certain areas because it is just too difficult to handle or because it would nudge you to change a behavior or attitude that you find some pleasure in?

☐ **FINDING OUR WAY**

Renewing the mind is different from renewing a subscription to a magazine. There is nothing new about the latter at all, just a continuation of the same. It is more like "expiration protection": another lap around the same track. Renewing the mind may require returning to some familiar territory, but along a different road. It's like taking a different path through the same woods or traveling the same highway in a different season of the year. It begins with a heart and mind that is open to the truth of Jesus.

Read Matthew 13:51-52.

10. Describe the payoff for those who seek truth with open hearts and minds, letting Jesus bring renewal.

☐ **PRAYING TOGETHER**

Ask God to soften your heart and to help you understand his deeper teachings with humility. Seek his renewing work.

☐ **CONSIDER THIS**

What kinds of practices or experiences might invite the renewal of your mind? Here are some ideas to prompt your thinking:

- meditation on sections of the Bible
- spending time with someone who has followed Jesus many years
- serving a church in another place and culture
- reading spiritual writings from great men and women of God
- a personal or group prayer retreat

What would you like to try?

THREE

Jesus

EXPOSES OUR MOTIVES

Knowing their thoughts, Jesus said . . .

☐ GATHERING TO LISTEN

A four-year-old named Ryan had a knack for getting what he wanted while making other kids feel very good for giving it to him. It would go something like this.

"Michael, these are really nice cars, huh?"

"Yeah, and I want to play with the blue one."

"Okay, Michael, you can have whichever car you want. If you want me to have the *really cool* red car, that's fine. It actually looks faster than the other one, though maybe not. But it sure looks great. And, of course, red is one of the best colors a car could be. Lots of people like red cars, and lots of red cars are fast. So if you want me to have it, that would be great, but it doesn't matter. Both cars look like they are fun."

Little Michael is now in a quandary—he has chosen the blue car, but how can he pass up a car that might be better and faster and cooler?

"Uh, I changed my mind. I want the red car," says Michael, smiling coyly as he snatches up the little racer as if he has just made the deal of the century.

"Okay," says Ryan without expression, "the blue car is just fine with me. And you have a really cool red car, huh, Michael? So now we each have a good car, right?"

"Yeah, we *each* do. Vroooommm!"

It was clear little Ryan had an agenda. And he did quite a good job at hiding that agenda when he wanted to get his way. He had a heart of gold (still does today at age sixteen); he would never intentionally hurt anyone. I should know—he's my son. Many of his actions at age four were commendable. But his craftiness in situations like this one could become damaging if it drifted over to the dark side of shrewdness—manipulation. If you are manipulative, soon your hidden agenda will be exposed, and your friends will be few.

Few of our actions stem from pure motives. As in little Ryan's case in this story, there may be dark motives behind what we do. We may manage our image with great care, but at the heart level resides an ever-present agenda of self-preservation. If we are honest, we can recall times we had a hidden agenda in mind.

- Why is it so hard to keep our motives pure? Why are we tempted to hide what is really going on?

☐ ENCOUNTERING JESUS

There was something wonderfully uncomfortable about being near Jesus. His teaching and expressions of healing and compassion drew all but the most hardhearted to his side. But once you were there, you knew that his love for you demanded that he tell you the truth about yourself.

Read Mark 9:33-37.

Jesus and his followers (disciples) return to Capernaum, Jesus' base of operations while he is in the Galilean region of Palestine. Along the way, a heated discussion has erupted over who is the greatest.

1. How does it feel to know that Jesus can peer into your heart and expose your motives?

2. From what you know of the disciples, what might prompt them to have this argument?

3. It's a sad reality that lots of family arguments take place on the road to church services. But when we walk into the building, an amazing change in demeanor takes place. How is that similar to what is happening in verses 33-34?

4. Jesus the provocative teacher challenges his followers with a counterintuitive approach. Instead of scolding them by saying something like "Arguing is sin" or with "Your pride is offensive to God, so let's put an end to this right now!" he communicates in a *more* unsettling way. Jesus asks a question. Why use a question instead of a straight rebuke?

☐ Joining the Conversation

Jesus gets at the heart of the issue now. Turning their thinking upside down, he describes a revolutionary approach to leadership. The last shall be first. The leader must be the servant, because Jesus is first and foremost a servant.

5. Where do you find the "last shall be first" servants in your life?

    • on the job

    • at the dinner table

    • at religious gatherings

    • at professional sporting events

    • in your group

    Describe someone you know who is a servant.

6. Observe the context of this event. Read Mark 9:30-32. What strikes you about the disciples' argument in light of what Jesus has just been saying about himself in verses 30-32?

☐ **CONNECTING OUR STORIES**

7. Using a child as a living illustration and word picture, Jesus explains that to welcome a child in his name is the same as welcoming God! What comes to mind as you realize that welcoming others is the same as welcoming God?

8. How are the themes of welcoming and servanthood related?

9. Take a moment and reflect on how your group could serve others through the discipline of welcoming. What shift in your thinking must take place for you to embrace welcoming as a lifestyle?

☐ FINDING OUR WAY

10. Jesus has exposed the disciples' (and our) deepest motive: self-preservation, instead of selfless servanthood. How do we move from self-preservation to servanthood?

11. Are you willing to do this even if there may be suffering involved, as there was for Jesus? Explain your response.

☐ PRAYING TOGETHER

Begin with a period of introspection and silent meditation on Mark 10:44-45. Allow Jesus, the servant who was willing to suffer, to meet you in those words. Sit in his presence and experience his grace.

You may want to thank him for his pure motives in serving you and others. Ask him to work in you to make your heart-level motivations more like his and to expose them when they drift toward selfishness.

☐ CONSIDER THIS

How might our group model this servant approach? Is there somewhere or someone we can serve as a group or individually in the next two weeks? A ministry in our church? A group of needy people in our city? A single mother?

FOUR

Jesus

CONFRONTS OUR UNBELIEF

Blessed are those who have not seen and yet have believed.

☐ **GATHERING TO LISTEN**

Astronauts from the USA have never landed on the moon.

The Holocaust is an exaggeration.

No one will ever want a computer on their desk.

Pharmaceutical companies do not want you healthy.

All men are liars.

No purchase necessary.

Honest, she's really cute.

Your check is in the mail.

No salesman will ever call.

Just send this form in and you'll get your rebate.

Never trust anyone over thirty.

- Look over the list above and comment on statements that make
  you laugh or cringe. What personal experiences make these statements particularly poignant, amusing or upsetting?

☐ **ENCOUNTERING JESUS**

Our world is filled with misrepresentation and lies. Scam artists abound, and any remaining remnants of trust are eroding rapidly. Whom can you believe these days? Even God is on trial. Can we trust God?

Mark Buchanan writes in *Your God Is Too Safe,* "The depth of our doubt is roughly proportional to the depth of our faith. Those with strong faith have equally strong doubt. . . . People with a trivial and shallow faith usually have trivial and shallow doubts." Makes you wonder.

Doubt drives the adventure of faith. No doubts, no room for faith. So Jesus confronts our doubts and our unbelief to draw out the emerging yet still dormant faith hidden beneath the layers of our fear, guilt and shame.

Read Mark 9:14-29.

1. Everyone has a reaction to Jesus (note verses 15 and 20). What impressions do you have of Jesus and of the situation in this story?

2. Focus on verses 14-19 and try to put yourself in the scene. In three or four words each, describe what might be the thoughts or feelings of each group or person below.
   - teachers of the law
   - Jesus, Peter, James and John
     as they return from the mountain
   - the young boy
   - the crowd
   - the disciples who couldn't
     drive out the spirit
   - the boy's father

3. As the father describes the boy's condition (something like epilepsy), try to imagine that he is your son. What is going through your mind?

4. To put this interaction in context, quickly look at Mark 3:13-15 and Mark 6:12-13. Why is Jesus so bitterly disappointed with his disciples?

☐ JOINING THE CONVERSATION

5. Jesus refers to the disciples as an "unbelieving generation." They are reminders of the ongoing resistance of people who have seen the work of God yet still do not believe. Think of people you know. Are we becoming "an unbelieving generation"?

6. This account recounts an interaction between Jesus and the unseen forces of darkness. In recent years demonic beings and forces have been the subject of many movies and science-fiction novels. Many people assume they are the stuff of myth. But here the Bible tells of a real encounter with an evil spirit. What do you notice about the encounter?

7. Do you believe that evil spirits are at work today? If so, what difference does that belief make to your life and your understanding of events? If not, to what do you attribute the strong presence of evil in the world?

Encountering evil spirits and demonic forces was normal for Jesus. Immediately after he began his public ministry, Satan tempted him to exchange God's will for his own. This was only the beginning of the spiritual battles that would be waged in the life and ministry of Jesus.

The increase and intensity in demonic activity surrounding Jesus in Palestine led his enemies to declare that he was possessed (see Luke 11:14-28; John 8:48-59 and 10:19-21). When the influence of Christ is present the activity of Satan intensifies.

Yet each time Jesus encounters a demon, he casts it out or destroys it. Those who follow Jesus can be assured that they are protected by his power.

☐ **CONNECTING OUR STORIES**

8. As the evil spirit controls the boy and throws him into a fit, Jesus pauses to ask the father a question (verse 21). Why would Jesus start this conversation with the father while the boy is convulsing?

9. In what ways are we all like the father in verses 23-24?

☐ **FINDING OUR WAY**

10. Look again at the people in this story. Each has a chance to respond

to Jesus. Some responses are recounted in the text, while others we can guess.

- The father comes with his son, hoping for healing yet not fully convinced.
- The evil spirit comes to destroy the life that God had created.
- The disciples cannot seem to grasp the deeper spiritual conflict.
- The crowd grows because Jesus is there, but do they just want to see another miracle?
- The teachers of the law are very far from home, and they are no friend to Jesus. Are they on a reconnaissance mission, seeking information to accuse him with?
- The son is likely fearful and ashamed, knowing he may suddenly convulse uncontrollably and not sure what his future holds—will he always be this way?

Now, how about you? What is your response to Jesus? Are you in the crowd—a curious onlooker? Are you like the father, whose faith is growing but uncertain? Or, like the disciples, are you having difficulty seeing the deeper spiritual realities that surround you?

11. Jesus makes it clear that prayer is the key to winning a spiritual battle. Where are you being challenged to step out with your fragile faith, and how might prayer play a role in the adventure?

"Enemy occupied territory—that is what the world is." Those words from C. S. Lewis should rattle us a bit. We must awaken to the reality that spiritual forces are at work, seeking to keep us from trusting in God's awesome power to change lives.

Perhaps your faith, like most of ours, is two parts unbelief, one part ambivalence and a pinch of trust. Don't underestimate that little pinch; faith as small as a mustard seed is all it takes, according to Jesus. Like courage, which cannot operate without fear, faith requires doubt to release it.

☐ PRAYING TOGETHER

Identify areas of doubt and fear in your life. Tell others in the group about them. Pray together for courage to act in the face of unbelief.

☐ CONSIDER THIS

Praying alone is a good spiritual discipline in times that you are away from community life. But do not neglect praying together, for where two or three are gathered for the purposes of Jesus, he is working among you.

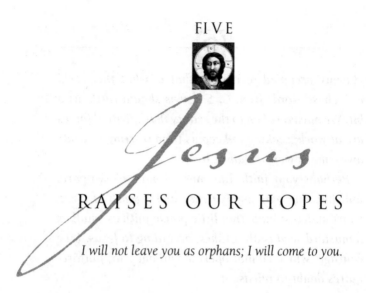

FIVE

Jesus

RAISES OUR HOPES

I will not leave you as orphans; I will come to you.

☐ **GATHERING TO LISTEN**

The Bible is filled with hope. Just look at some of the hope-filled words God has given us.

> In this world you will have trouble. But take heart! I have overcome the world. (John 16:33)

> Neither death nor life . . . can separate us from the love of God that is in Christ Jesus our Lord. (Romans 8:38-39)

> There is now no condemnation for those who are in Christ Jesus. (Romans 8:1)

> When you are tempted, he will also provide a way out so that you can stand up under it. (1 Corinthians 10:13)

> He alone is my rock and my salvation; he is my fortress, I will not be shaken. (Psalm 62:6)

> Though outwardly we are wasting away, yet inwardly we are being renewed day by day. (2 Corinthians 4:16)

I sought the LORD, and he answered me; he delivered me from all my fears. (Psalm 34:4)

So that, having been justified by his grace, we might become heirs having the hope of eternal life . . . (Titus 3:7)

And surely I am with you always, to the very end of the age. (Matthew 28:20)

- As you read these passages from the Bible, what internal reaction occurs? Which ones do you feel more deeply today? Why?

☐ **ENCOUNTERING JESUS**

In the passage we will read, we find Jesus with the disciples, eating the Passover feast with them. He tells them that he will be going away (to the cross and to his death) and they cannot make this journey with him. Sensing their fear and confusion at his pending departure, he begins to give them comfort and hope, saying, "Do not let your hearts be troubled. Trust in God; trust also in me. In my Father's house are many rooms; if it were not so, I would have told you. I am going there to prepare a place for you. And if I go to prepare a place for you, I will come back and take you to be with me that you also may be where I am" (John 14:1-3).

Read John 14:15-31.

1. Take a moment and write down every promise Jesus makes and every word of encouragement he gives in these few verses.

2. What do you notice about Jesus as he makes these statements?

What insights do you have about his relationship with the disciples and his mission in the world?

☐ JOINING THE CONVERSATION

> *Jewish people in Jesus' day put their hope and trust in God. That was what their ancestors had done, as recorded in the Torah and in the psalms and hymns of Israel. They hoped for a deliverer—a Messiah—to come and free them from Roman oppression.*

3. In light of messianic hopes, what kinds of thoughts might be running through the disciples' minds as they hear these words?

4. Though Jesus is leaving, his presence will remain. The Holy Spirit will come. According to these verses, what is the role and ministry of the Spirit?

How will the Spirit encourage the disciples in the absence of Jesus?

5. Jesus says he will make his home with us. How can this be if he is leaving? (See verses 18-23.)

6. Obedience to the Father's mission is central for Jesus. What is this mission, and how will it be fulfilled?

☐ **CONNECTING OUR STORIES**

7. As you think of your life, what hopes do you hold for the future?

8. What events or trends in our world threaten to destroy your hopes and dreams?

In verses 28-29 Jesus is not speaking in a snide way as a teenage girl might say to her mother, "If you really loved me, you'd let me go to the prom with Brandon!" Jesus is mildly rebuking the disciples for the shallowness of their love and their lack of understanding of his greater mission. They should be glad, in some sense, that his mission is being accomplished, as marked by his return to the Father. They have a short-term view and are more concerned with losing his friendship. To love Jesus fully is to love his mission.

What would you do if every dream you had was shattered?

9. How might the call of God on your life—his mission for you—affect your dreams?

☐ **FINDING OUR WAY**

10. Are your hopes placed in God and his purposes? If not, are you interested in discovering living a purpose God has set before you? Or are you focused on fulfilling your dreams through work, investment strategies or fitness goals? What would it look like to place all our hope in God, and how might that change the way we choose to live?

☐ **PRAYING TOGETHER**

Desperate, fearful, sick, lonely and confused people need hope. Those of us who think we have it all together, however, rarely feel such a need. In order to be hope-filled people, we must acknowledge that this present world has little to offer us, and we must admit that we are actually needy and broken. We need the presence and life of Christ in us. We need the power of God, working through his Spirit, to meet the challenges we face and to calm our fears.

In this dependent state of mind we seek God, our only hope.

Read Psalm 33:16-22 through once. Pause and reflect. Then try paraphrasing each verse as a personal prayer. For example, verse 16 might be rephrased, "God, I know that no one is saved by their own power and skill. This is true of me; I cannot escape the evil in this world in my own strength. None of us can."

SIX

Jesus

PRODS OUR TRANSFORMATION

Unless you change and become like children,
you will never enter the kingdom of heaven.

☐ **GATHERING TO LISTEN**

There are certain laws that cannot be ignored. Unless they are followed, you will run into major trouble. Here are a few "laws" of golf that are as certain as snow in a Chicago winter.

Your best round of golf will be followed by your worst round ever.

New golf balls contain a water magnet, no matter where you aim.

No matter what you did to muff a shot, your partners will always chant, "You looked up."

Every par 3 hole is designed so that you get a 6.

The last three holes of a round will automatically adjust your score to what it really should be.

When you accidentally hit your ball into another group of golfers, it will always include an ex-football player, a wrestler and an IRS agent.

The more expensive the ball, the more likely you will lose it.

The more expensive the green fee, the worse your score will be.

And finally—you will always get a hole in one the day you play alone and there is no one else playing within five hundred yards of you.

- Our world is filled with unalterable laws that must be obeyed or we feel the consequences. The law of gravity is one of those. Name some others (serious or humorous) and how they affect your life.

□ **ENCOUNTERING JESUS**

Jesus is about to unfold one of the laws by which his kingdom operates. It is one of those counterintuitive principles that can make your head spin. Spiritual transformation—true life change—is dependent on this law. And it is one of the most difficult to obey.

Read Matthew 18:1-9.

1. What do you think is prompting the question asked by the disciples in Matthew 18:1?

2. How does Jesus define true greatness?

How do you think the disciples receive his words?

3. According to verses 3-4, what is this kingdom-of-heaven law?

   What is the first thing that impresses you about this law?

   How is it countercultural?

4. Why would Jesus give such a stern warning in verse 6?

☐ JOINING THE CONVERSATION

5. *Read 1 Peter 5:5.* From 1 Peter and Matthew 18, how would you describe the kind of person God seeks to work in?

   What kind of person does he oppose?

6. How do the personality qualities God is looking for compare with what is valued in most work environments in our society?

Humility is the foundation of all spiritual transformation, because we cannot change ourselves. We need outside help to accomplish an inside job. When several rooms of our house needed painting, I hired someone to do the job. I'm no expert. Whether it's a tax return, an engine tune-up, delivering a talk to three thousand people or designing a new home, there are some things we need experts for. When it comes to transformation, the Bible is clear. It is a work of God (see Philippians 1:6) that we cannot do alone. Yes, we are in partnership with that work (see Philippians 2:12) and are responsible to obey, yield and step out in faith. But it's a God thing. And it requires a humble heart.

7. Take a moment to check your humility factor. Use the scale below.

    1 = I rise each day asking God to show me how I can serve him and others in my life.

    2 = Most of the time I have an attitude of submission and willingness to learn.

    3 = I begin each day with a desire to follow God but soon discover that I like being independent and self-motivated.

    4 = I don't need any more "humiliation" in my life, and I see no need to get stepped on all day, so I have taken control of my own life.

    5 = If anyone threatens my agenda or success, I will squash him like a bug and splatter his remains on the sidewalk of my life!

    (**Note:** If you checked number 5, please leave the meeting now and call 1-800-LOCK-ME-UP at your earliest convenience.)

    What have you discovered about yourself?

8. Jesus is serious about the extreme danger of causing others to sin. Take a few moments to consider why he has such a view. How would you define *sin*?

9. Why do you think Jesus suddenly turns from his discussion of humility to the topic of sinning against "these little ones"? (Note that "these little ones" are probably not little children.) How are these topics related?

CONNECTING OUR STORIES

10. Jesus uses a strong word of judgment, "Woe," and some exaggeration (a style known as *hyperbole*) in verses 7-9 to make his point stick. Again, he is serious about the effects of sin. If we cause ourselves or other followers of Jesus to stumble, we are going to be judged. As you think of your life and of others in the group, what is Jesus trying to protect you from?

11. Take a few quiet moments to reflect on the sins that keep you from living the kingdom life Jesus desires for you. There's no need to discuss them with anyone. Hear the voice of Jesus saying, "Give those to me and I will take care of them—I have better plans for you. Stop

holding on to stuff that you think gives you pleasure and security. Let go, and I will show you how to really live!" What attitudes do these words evoke in you as you read them? Why?

☐ Finding Our Way

12. Humility is the pathway to spiritual growth. Pride is a barrier to life change. Based on what has been discussed, what needs to change so that we can grow?

☐ Praying Together

Take time to confess prideful attitudes and selfish motives. Ask God to show you when you start to power up over others or when you are becoming the focus of attention. Consider using Colossians 3:12-17 as a prayer guide.

☐ Consider This

Get together this week with one or two other group members to discuss what you have learned over the past six weeks.

NOTES FOR LEADERS

Each session has a similar format using the components below. Here is a very rough guide for the amount of time you might spend on each segment for a ninety-minute meeting time, excluding additional social time. This is a general guide, and you will learn to adjust the format as you become comfortable working together as a group:

Gathering to Listen	5-10 minutes
Encountering Jesus	15 minutes
Joining the Conversation	20 minutes
Connecting Our Stories	20 minutes
Finding Our Way	10 minutes
Praying Together	about 10 minutes

You can take some shortcuts or take longer as the group decides, but strive to stay on schedule for a ninety-minute meeting including prayer time. You will also want to save time to attend to personal needs and prayer. This will vary by group and can also be accomplished in personal relationships you develop between meetings.

As group leader, know that you help create an environment for spiritual growth. Here are a few things to consider as you invite people to follow in the company of Jesus.

LEADER TIPS

Practice authenticity and truth telling. Do not pretend an elephant is not sitting in the middle of the room when everyone knows it is.

- Does your group have a commitment to pursue personal change and growth?
- Set some ground rules or a covenant for group interactions. Consider values like confidentiality, respect and integrity.
- Model and encourage healthy self-disclosure through icebreakers, storytelling and getting to know one another between meetings.

SESSION 1.
JESUS SHATTERS OUR ILLUSIONS.
Matthew 5:1-12

This session is designed to help people think differently about growth, helping them realize that often old structures need to be torn down before new ones are built. It is like remodeling an older home: some areas can be repainted, but others need to be restructured. Jesus' teaching is so different and revolutionary that he must often shatter the illusions we hold about how God works and how we relate to him.

Gathering to Listen (5-7 minutes). This is a story to which many people will relate. Focus here on an initial reaction to it. Members may express frustrations with work, with relationships or with their spiritual life. They may have illusions about God or the church and may express disappointments in these arenas. Here our focus is expression, not judgment or explanation.

Encountering Jesus (15 minutes). The Beatitudes introduce the Sermon on the Mount, Jesus' call to moral and ethical living in the kingdom of God. This section sets the tone for Jesus' teaching. Immediately he begins to teach in ways they have never heard before. His words are counterintuitive to the average hearer.

"Blessed" here refers to deep joy and well-being, not superficial happiness. The blessing is found not in their condition but in what that condition evokes. So the "poor in spirit" are blessed because "theirs is the kingdom." Their spiritual poverty, sometimes revealed through physical poverty, forces them to turn toward God. The kingdom is offered and the spiritually bankrupt are blessed as they receive the promises and person of the King, Jesus. (You may want to acknowledge that the "kingdom of God" metaphor can seem very alien in our world, where democracy is a high value. Let participants know that various facets of God's kingdom will be revealed throughout the course of your discussions; there's no need to understand it fully now.)

The "meek" inherit the new earth, (the new promised land described in Revelation 21:1) because of their humble disposition toward God. People who exercise gentleness and humility in the sight of God are fit to participate in life in the eternal kingdom, the new heaven and new earth.

The "pure in heart" will see God because of a single-minded devotion to his ways and his lifestyle—purity, honor, justice, integrity. As one develops this kind of heart, one sees the things of God—and God himself—more clearly.

"Peacemakers" are called sons of God because, as God's children, they reflect the heart of Jesus, the "Prince of Peace" (Isaiah 9:6). We are more than simply peace lovers, we are called to be peacemakers who promote reconciliation among human beings and between God and people through Christ (2 Corinthians 5). Peacemaking does not mean passivity. Peacemakers are initiators, often entering into a conflict and taking the risks associated with the work of reconciliation.

All of these "Blessed are" statements are designed to provoke people—to call them out to deeper understanding of the kingdom perspective on life. Those who seek after the kingdom of God and the ways of Jesus are truly blessed.

Joining the Conversation (20 minutes). A worldview is the result of life experiences, assumptions we hold, teaching we have soaked in, patterns of relating we have developed. Take a moment here to guide the discussion toward self-disclosure. Encourage your small group community to listen and understand, not judge or preach. We are simply trying to understand ourselves and others in our group.

Connecting Our Stories (20 minutes). We naturally begin to link our own stories with the story of the Bible. The questions here are designed to create some tension. Don't be concerned about disagreement. The point is to find out how we are engaging with Jesus' story. We have now encountered him as provocative teacher—what does that mean to us? Each of us has a view of the world. Now Jesus is breaking in on that view, challenging our assumptions and clarifying the ways in which his kingdom operates. What does that mean for our relationships in this group?

Encourage members to express freely how the teaching of Jesus is affecting them. Do they see him differently now that they "hear" him teach?

As you discuss question 7, take a little time to understand the spiritual heritage (or lack thereof) of your fellow group members.

Finding Our Way (10 minutes). Prompt participants to consider changes in attitudes and activities as a result of encountering this illusion-shattering Jesus. What actions or activities may result from this encounter?

Praying Together (about 10 minutes). Consider praying in smaller groups of two or three people so that members can share their insights and prayer needs. If this is your first meeting, spend some time getting to know each other. Be sensitive to members for whom group prayer is awkward or new. Perhaps you could ask them to join you in a little subgroup, so that you can make their initial experience with prayer meaningful and personal. Give them freedom to pray aloud but don't pressure them to do so.

SESSION 2.
JESUS RENEWS OUR MIND.
Matthew 13:1-23, 51-52.

Gathering to Listen (5-10 minutes). Look for common themes in people's stories that may emerge. Perhaps group members have a common experience related to fresh starts in life. Or you may encounter someone who was part of a cult or had a rigid upbringing. When they got out of it, it was like a new day. But they may have quickly realized the level of manipulation or mind control others had exercised over them. Now they must renew their mind.

Encountering Jesus (15 minutes). Jesus uses the power of a story, a parable, to initially connect with his audience. Using common, earthy realities familiar to his culture, Jesus draws an analogy that unveils for us some kingdom mysteries. For more on how to understand parables, see *Parables and Prophecy: Unlocking the Bible's Mysteries* in IVP's Bible 101 study series. Remember, we are encountering Jesus as a teacher of truth. His ways are often countercultural.

The point in this section is to allow participants to express any confusion about why Jesus would teach in order to "hide" truth from people. Since this is such one of the more challenging passages in the Bible, here's some extra background help on verses 11-15.

Verse 11. First, let's get clear on who the "you" and the "them" are. At this point we are not sure, but soon Jesus will explain that those who harden their hearts cannot repent and receive truth that God has revealed. So "them" cannot mean everyone except the disciples. Verse 9 also provides a clue. Those with ears—that is, those with heart and mind open to God's message—will hear. Jesus is saying something like "Come, you kingdom seekers! Listen and learn!"

We see this principle at work in Matthew 3:2, where John the Baptizer says, "Repent, for the kingdom of heaven is near." John says that God's kingdom is breaking onto the scene and will be fully revealed when Jesus, the King, comes. Notice, however, that repentance (softening of the heart and turning toward God) is required to embrace the kingdom.

Verse 12. "Whoever has more." More what? The same phrase is used in Matthew 25:29 in the context of the parable of the talents. The one who was given "more" in that teaching is the one who faithfully invests his five talents and earns five more for the master. He is later entrusted with more—more to manage and steward because of his faithfulness.

So here, in our passage, "more" appears to be more openness to God's truth, more humility, greater ability to handle the truth wisely and faithfully. But Jesus couches the truth in a parable so that seekers find while the rebellious—those who cannot or will not receive his words—remain blind to it. That will prevent them from misusing or mishandling the truth.

Verse 15. Using this quote from Isaiah, Jesus is reminding hearers that there is judgment for the hardhearted who reject God. Despite many opportunities to repent, Israel continued in disobedience and suffered the judgment of God. The same is true for those with ears that no longer hear and process truth because of hardened hearts and closed eyes.

Think of it this way. For the last three days you have not done your homework for English class. You have rejected the teaching of the professor. Twice she has warned you that it will affect your grade for the course. To make her point, she walks to the board and begins using vocabulary words and illustrations from readings you have not done. You are confused.

She is intentionally using words from the assignments in order to develop the understanding of the students who have faithfully done their homework. At the same time, she is "hiding" the teaching from you by not explaining the terms she is using. Nor does she review the stories she makes allusions to. After all, you are supposed to have read those stories.

She asks you a few questions, but you are unable to answer. So what is your response? A wise student would humble himself and seek help from the teacher. He would acknowledge he was wrong for neglecting the work and her teaching. He would ask for another chance to catch up and join the rest of the class.

But a rebellious student would think, *So you're trying to embarrass me! Fine! Now I am not reading anything! Go ahead, ask me more questions. See if I care! I won't even try to answer. After all, English is stupid and your teaching is boring!*

Rebellious Israel had responded in much the same way to God and to his messengers, hardening their hearts and becoming increasingly unreceptive to truth.

Joining the Conversation (20 minutes). With these questions let's seek to make the link between the mind and the heart. Mind renewal is a heart condition. Ephesians 4:17-24 will help you see this more clearly. Notice Ephesians 4:18: "They are darkened in their understanding and separated from the life of God because of the ignorance that is in them due to the hardening of their hearts." It may be helpful to look at this passage with your group to clarify further the connection of heart and mind.

In what way are God's people ignorant today to his ways? Do you know such people? Are their hearts open or closed?

"Prophets and righteous men" of the Old Testament era longed to see the full expression of the kingdom of God, ushered in by the coming Messiah. But they died before the coming of Christ. The disciples are truly blessed because they see the fulfillment firsthand.

Connecting Our Stories (20 minutes). Try to get beyond initial reactions to Jesus' teaching and ask each person to look at their own heart and mind. Are we thinking rightly about truth and transformation? Are we clear about the connection between heart and mind? Help group members understand that their ability to process truth with the mind is related to the receptivity of the heart.

You may have to lead the way here, especially because the questions require a deeper level of self-disclosure and honesty. Members are being asked to identify areas of life where they might need a softer heart and open mind. By sharing first you will encourage others to tell some of their story. But always be sensitive to members. There is a difference between probing and pushing.

You might try this portion of the meeting in groups of two or three so that participants feel safer talking about their heart and about areas they need to open up to the truth and work of God. At first this may feel awkward. But as people get to know one another, they tend to connect with one or two members that they feel more comfortable with, so give it some time.

Finding Our Way (10 minutes). Jesus explains the parable quite clearly.

The four kinds of soil (some call this "the parable of the soils") represent four kinds of hearts, four levels of receptivity to the message of the kingdom. At first there is no distinction among the soils. The sower does not sow the seed any differently. It all looks the same from a distance as he throws the seed over a wide area. He hopes and expects it will all settle in and take root, yielding a productive crop. But quickly Jesus makes it clear that soil conditions are different out in the field. And this is the determining factor.

The four responses are clear. It is the fourth kind of soil (the heart of a receptive, kingdom-seeking person) that is able to not only receive the seed but to bring it to full fruition.

Spend some time pondering the payoff of having our minds renewed by Jesus. What will it look like to have a life that yields a crop thirty, sixty or a hundred times what was sown? Do we all want that kind of fruitfulness in our spiritual life? If so, what does that mean? What must change? What would such a life look like? This is the focus of question 10.

Praying Together. You might try a different kind of prayer here. If your group is more established and maturing, try reading through Ephesians 3:14-21 or Colossians 1:9-14 together. Pause after each phrase or section of the prayer and meditate on it together. Try paraphrasing the words and personalizing it for your group.

Once again, notice how the heart and mind are referred to in the prayer. This kind of prayer will reinforce what you just discovered together.

Consider This. This section is designed to generate ideas. You might take a few minutes to brainstorm as a group. What could be done to help stretch and renew your mind as it relates to Jesus and his ways? For example, it may be getting to know each group member more deeply, discovering their story. This will make you more receptive to both God's truth and the truth about them.

SESSION 3.
JESUS EXPOSES OUR MOTIVES.
Mark 9:33-37

Gathering to Listen (7-8 minutes). This story about a child reveals how mixed our motives may be. We want to be better but must acknowledge that much of what we do is designed to serve ourselves—even when making others feel good.

Prompt the group to consider the emphasis on "self-preservation" that exists in our culture. There are whole industries devoted to this, whether in the area of fitness, beauty, finances or employment. How do we fight upstream against it? What part of this self-preservation focus is healthy, and when does it cross the line?

Encountering Jesus (15 minutes). The Bible says of Jesus, "He knew all people and needed no one to testify about anyone; for he himself knew what was in everyone" (John 2:24-25 NRSV). Look also at Matthew 9:4 and 12:25. He knows the thoughts of people and what is in their hearts. So getting close to Jesus means not simply getting to know *him* better but getting to see *yourself* more fully—whether you want to or not. That can be very uncomfortable.

Capernaum was the base of operations for Jesus and his disciples when they were ministering in Galilee. Some suggest the home mentioned here was possibly the home of Peter and Andrew that Jesus frequented (see Mark 1:29). It must have been the place for many a small group meeting and some intense meal sharing. It was an environment for the group to debrief ministry activity, rest, connect and be taught by Jesus (and fed by Peter's mother!).

Jesus did much of his discipleship using questions. He used different kinds of questions for different occasions:

- rhetorical questions whose answer is already known: "What good is it for a man to gain the whole world, yet forfeit his soul?" (Mark 8:36)
- open-ended questions: "Who do people say the Son of Man is?" (Matthew 16:13)
- information questions: "What do you want me to do for you?" (Mark 10:36)
- judgment questions, challenging sinful attitudes or behaviors: "Which is lawful on the Sabbath: to do good or to do evil, to save life or to destroy it?" (Luke 6:9)
- introspective questions, forcing people to examine themselves: "What were you arguing about on the road?" (Mark 9:33)

Here Jesus is using a question to cause his followers to look inward, where their conscience and the convicting ministry of the Spirit are at work. In this way he is gentle but at the same time firmly confronts their pride. The guilt and shame of the disciples is rebuke enough, and Jesus lets his simple question sink in and do its work. It has much more power than an open rebuke in this case, though the disciples deserved a scolding. Such a question opens the door for change. You could say to your son, "I told you never to take the car keys without asking me first!" Or you could say, "What was going through your mind when you took the keys without asking me first, as we had agreed?" Each may be appropriate in different circumstances. Here Jesus opts for a probing question.

Joining the Conversation (20 minutes). The disciples have been arguing about greatness, and you can cut the irony with a knife. Jesus has just finished some rather remarkable miracles, and he has just been teaching the disciples about how he must suffer and die (10:30-32). Yet they dismiss this, and then, almost without thought to Jesus or the suffering that lies ahead for him, they argue about who is greatest.

This would be like seeing *The Passion of the Christ,* a gut-wrenching depiction of the bloody torture and crucifixion of Jesus, and then saying, "Where are we going for ice cream?" It is unthinkable. But that is what the disciples have just done.

Help participants see the countercultural call to servanthood and humility that Jesus extends to all his followers. We live in a "What have you done for me lately?" world. But Jesus is interested in an other-oriented mindset, a welcoming attitude toward outsiders who are not yet in the kingdom. To welcome little ones in his name is to welcome God.

Connecting Our Stories (20 minutes). Jean Vanier, in his book *Community and Growth,* says, "A loving community is attractive, and a community that is attractive is by definition welcoming. Life brings new life. . . . A community which refuses to welcome—whether through fear, weariness, insecurity, a desire to cling to comfort, or just because it is fed up with visitors—is dying spiritually."

Consider reading the quote above and asking for members to react and consider their own heart and attitudes toward welcoming others, toward having kingdom motives versus personal motives for their actions.

You might also draw attention to the familiar teaching of Jesus that the one who serves the needy serves him (Matthew 25:31-46). In this way we welcome God as we welcome others.

In Jesus' day, children were not given attention in spiritual discussions. Such discussions were to take place at home. Even the disciples tried to keep them away at one point, and Jesus rebuked them (Matthew 19:13-14).

Finding Our Way (10 minutes). To help the group move increasingly from selfish motives to unselfish ones, investigate a serving opportunity. Actions will speak louder than words. To discuss servanthood is one thing; to serve is another. Seek to serve the poor, orphans, widows, single parents, newcomers to the community, members of minority groups, children in need. Brainstorm together—and then commit to some kind of action before the meeting ends.

Praying Together (about 10 minutes). This is similar to the prayer of examen, which has been used by many Christians throughout history as a means of asking God to purify their hearts and expose wrong beliefs, attitudes or motives. This reflection can be done for five minutes as you ponder Mark 10:44-45. Then move into other kinds of prayer as desired and as the Spirit leads you.

SESSION 4.
JESUS CONFRONTS OUR UNBELIEF.
Mark 9:14-29

Gathering to Listen (5-10 minutes). These statements are designed to stir memories of participants as they identify the cynicism and unbelief in our society. You can use this as a discussion starter and spend more time discussing the various responses, especially if new people are joining the group. Take time to get to know each other more through people's responses.

Encountering Jesus (15 minutes). Everyone had a reaction to Jesus. His teaching and actions created quite a stir. Help group members put themselves in the shoes of those in the story. You might even assign roles and ask participants to take one or two minutes to jot down what they might be thinking or feeling as father, son, teacher of the law and so on. Keep this brief and get an initial reaction, just three or four words that come to mind.

Now, in question 2 try to help them see the story at a deeper, personal level. The boy is *your* son. What are you hoping for Jesus to do? Why did you bring him there in the first place? Remember the boy has been ill since birth, so his condition has lasted five years, ten years or more. In what condition is such a father? Tired, at wits' end, filled with pity, hopeless?

Note the frustration the father expresses in verse 19. He had trusted the disciples to heal his son, but they could not. Soon Jewish leaders were pointing out this failure and challenging the disciples. So what fueled the argument? Had the disciples promised to heal the boy and then could not, and were therefore rebuked by the teachers of the law? Were they arguing that they really did have power to heal while the lawyers remained unconvinced?

In any case, Jesus arrived with Peter, James and John and soon discovered the failure. His frustration rose because whatever the disciples had not done they should have been able to do by now. After all, they had been given power to cast out evil spirits (Mark 3:13-15) and had done so before (Mark 6:12-13). Maybe they got cocky, or maybe they defaulted to some kind of formula. *If we just say, "In Jesus' name!" and wave our hand, he will be delivered.*

Joining the Conversation (20 minutes). Unbelief is widespread in the world, even among those who know and have seen the hand of God. It is easy to explain away. People look for signs as if to say "show us again!" This frustrated Jesus. He wanted changed hearts and the love of the Father to be enough for people to see that God was at work. Miracles were done to authenticate his power but were not intended to be the dominant method for establishing relationships with people. They were one way—among many—to demonstrate the love of God and his compassion for people in need.

Look at Luke 11:14-16 and John 2:18 for examples of people who kept seeking signs even though Jesus had performed many. When our belief is centered primarily on miracles, our faith remains shallow. "Blessed are they who have not seen and yet have believed," said Jesus to Thomas after he had touched the wounds of the resurrected Christ (John 20:29).

The greatest evidence for belief is the changing of a human heart. In this story, everyone but Jesus seems to miss that fact. Jesus wants to heal the boy—but he also wants to strengthen the faith of the father. So there are two healings here.

Take some time with questions 6 and 7 to check in with the group about their belief or understanding of the reality of evil. Remember September 11, 2001, atrocities committed in the Democratic Republic of Congo and the Sudan, the neglect and abuse of children, slavery and the selling of young girls into prostitution. Such happenings around the world give strong evidence to the presence of an evil so dark that it is hard to explain apart from the existence of evil forces. If there is not an evil one (or demons, evil spirits, etc.) and human beings are basically good, how do we account for the prevalence of this activity?

The point here is to let the Bible speak. Do not focus on proving others wrong. Let them ponder the story and what they see around the world. Allow people who disagree with a biblical viewpoint to express their questions and doubts without passing judgment on them.

A note about group process: Remind members that everything shared in a group will be respected. But also remind them that when opinions or ideas are verbalized, they are subject to evaluation and questioning. There is space for disagreements and contrary opinions to be expressed. So though we value all opinions, members have the freedom to disagree. As leader, make sure the exchange remains civil and honoring to all members.

Connecting Our Stories (20 minutes). It is curious that Jesus does not immediately heal the boy. Instead he asks the father a question. You might picture the boy writhing on the ground, yet Jesus is calmly making a diagnosis. Does he not know all things? Could he not simply heal the boy and get his medical history later? Let's look at these actions in light of what we know of Jesus and how he acts. Here are some examples.

When Lazarus is dying in John 11, Jesus appears to take his time getting there but then weeps at his tomb. He appears in no hurry to get to Jairus's house to heal his sick daughter, stopping along the way to deal with a woman who has touched his cloak and was healed in the process. He asks, "Who touched me?" and gets into a dialogue with the woman. You would think that because she is already healed he would just keep pushing through the crowd to get to the sick girl.

In each case, Jesus is healing at more than one level. He is raising the dead and healing the sick, but he seems equally concerned with changing hearts and building up people's *faith*—belief! "Your *faith* has healed you," he says to the woman who touched him, and "Don't be afraid; *just believe* and she will be healed" to Jairus concerning his daughter (Luke 8:40-56).

So here Jesus is taking the opportunity not only to heal a boy but to increase the faith of a father. This also provides a teaching moment for the crowd: "Everything is possible for him who believes" (Mark 9:23).

The focus is belief, so Jesus confronts the unbelief of everyone present—the teachers of the law, the father, the disciples and the crowd. Interestingly, the demons believe more readily than they (and we) do (see James 2:19 in reference to Mark 9:20).

Jesus knows we are more like the father than we care to admit. Oh, we believe—for a while. But quickly that belief seems to erode and weaken. At least the father is honest—he admits he is double-minded. And he asks for help regarding his faith, not just healing for his son. He has changed: he recognizes that Jesus alone can help him restore and build his faith.

Finding Our Way (10 minutes). Help members take a close look at their faith structure. Help them to take an honest look at how they view themselves in relation to God.

Emphasize that prayer—spiritual power—is required for spiritual battles. We live in enemy territory and are in conflict with spiritual forces. These are unseen but not unreal, invisible yet very influential, formidable but (thanks to Jesus) not indestructible. Jesus has secured a victory over sin and death, and prayer places his power at our disposal to meet the enemy and defeat him—every time (see Ephesians 6:10).

Praying Together. There is no need to overemphasize the spiritual battle, but we cannot ignore it and the influence evil can have on us personally and on our world. It is important to pray for protection from the divisive work of evil (John 17:11, 15) and to place our faith—the little we may have—in Jesus. Our small faith in his powerful hands can change the world.

SESSION 5.
JESUS RAISES OUR HOPES.
John 14:15-31

Gathering to Listen (15 minutes). These passages are a sampling of verses that elicit hope. You may feel like using or adding others that are meaningful to you or your group. Starting with Scripture will confront the group head-on with the hope of God. You may want to use an icebreaker question, especially with a newer group. For example: "Where in this world today do we find voices of hope?" Or, "Who speaks the most hope into your life these days?" Then read the passages from the Bible.

As you get reactions from members, use this as a time for community building. Some may be deeply moved by the verses; others may feel some despair and not have much hope in the moment. Pause for prayer and interaction here if necessary. Don't rush the agenda and miss the moment.

Encountering Jesus (15 minutes). Listing the promises and encouraging words of Jesus will quickly show how much hope and inspiration is being packed into this upper-room meeting. Jesus is giving his followers hope in many areas. If you want, you can guide the group to look at each of these areas that Jesus addresses:

- the Holy Spirit—who he is and what he does
- the disciples' future relationship with Jesus
- their relationship with the Father in heaven
- the role of Jesus' commands and teaching
- the state of the disciples' hearts
- the activity of the "prince of this world," Satan
- the importance and focus of Jesus' mission

If this takes extra time, you can adjust later. If members are engaging deeply with this material, don't short-circuit the process. Let the Bible do its work.

Jesus has a sensitive heart toward the disciples here, but he balances that with a mild rebuke and several challenges. He is able to show them both tender and tough love.

Joining the Conversation (20 minutes). Some further questions you could use to draw out responses to question 3:

- Do the disciples realize what is about to happen?
- Perhaps they see their dreams shattering, their hopes for a Messiah-hero to free them from Rome; are they wondering if they made a mistake by pinning their hopes on Jesus?

The hope for Messiah was the primary focus of God's people. Once John the Baptizer began his ministry, that anticipation would have risen. He was "preparing the way" (Matthew 3:3), and many were awakened to the possibility that Messiah might be coming soon. False messiahs abounded, to be sure, but the work of John was unique and created quite a stir.

Everyone wondered whether Jesus was the fulfillment of John's words. Now, after three years of being with Jesus, the disciples are still not clear on what he is really doing. Their expectations do not match Jesus' mission and methods. So perhaps they wonder, *Is this really the one?* Peter has already declared, "You are the Messiah of God," but the interactions in this upper-room meeting make us all wonder how deeply that had sunk in. Perhaps there were lingering hopes for an immediately political messiah.

The role of the Holy Spirit is partially spelled out by Jesus. In John 16:5-16 he will provide more details; for now we see that the Spirit is a counselor (an advocate, an adviser) to represent God and come to the aid of Jesus' followers. He is sent by the Father (and later we learn by the Son as well) to teach and bring to memory the words of Jesus.

Through the Holy Spirit (also called elsewhere in the Bible the "Spirit of Christ" and the "Spirit of God"—see Romans 8:9), the Father and Son will make their abiding presence known to every believer. This is God making his home with us.

Jesus' mission is the redemption of the world, achieved through his atoning sacrifice on the cross (in our place) and his satisfaction of the justice of God ("the LORD has laid on him the iniquity of us all," Isaiah 53:6). He is calling to himself a new community to reign with him and enjoy him forever.

Connecting Our Stories (20 minutes). In these questions we want to get members uncovering their personal hopes and dreams, thus identifying with the disciples. But the challenge is to also compare our own hopes and dreams with the plan and purposes of God. Some Christians do not distinguish between God's plans and their own dreams. We go our way, design a lifestyle we enjoy and then ask God to bless it. We may have put the dreams our culture puts before us in the place of the redemptive mission of God.

Allow time for people to wrestle with the tension between God's dream—a sacrificial life of following Jesus wherever he leads—and our personal dreams. There will be some typical questions: Are our dreams bad? Is it wrong to have some nice things? Do we all have to go to Africa to follow God? How do I know what God wants me to do?

Some of these may be beyond the scope of the meeting's discussion, but allow members to express their thoughts. The key is to raise the right questions: what does it mean to follow God in a world that is not very interested in supporting God's mission?

Finding Our Way (10 minutes). This final challenge is an alignment question: What will it take for me to align my life with God's purposes and mission? If God is calling us into his great work of helping people find him, how can I become a part of that? What might I need to stop or to avoid in the process of aligning my will with God's ways?

Encourage members to be honest about what they are really pinning their hopes on. A good test is always a look at how we use our time, spend our money and manage our relationships.

Praying Together. God's will is revealed in Scripture. That does not mean we should not pray for guidance to find his will; however, our prayers should focus on asking God to make us receptive and aware of his will. We ask him for courage to face hard decisions to align with his will. And we seek the power of the Spirit—our helper, comforter and counselor.

SESSION 6.
JESUS PRODS OUR TRANSFORMATION.
Matthew 18:1-9

Gathering to Listen (10 to 15 minutes). The purpose of these humorous golf laws is to allow people to have a little fun, because soon the discussion will become serious, taking up matters of humility and the consequences of sin. Jesus is telling us that transformation requires a change of heart, a humility that counters the selfish pride that generally sets the course for our life. As participants name various laws, ask why these are laws in the first place. What kind of person would have disregard for such laws? Fools despise laws, even laws that bring life and provide protection.

This will set up the discussion later of Jesus' law of spiritual transformation: Nothing happens without humility.

Encountering Jesus (15 minutes). The disciples ask the question because they have been debating this topic among themselves. The parallel passages in Mark 9:33-38 and Luke 9:46-48 are worth a quick read. If we link them together, it is likely that this question arises as a result of Jesus confronting them about their discussion. Pride and a worldly pursuit of greatness are at the core of their question.

Jesus counters this with a discussion of what true greatness is. By putting a child before them, he is not affirming childishness or even saying children are pure and innocent. Even little children sin. (If there are any doubts on this, I have a roomful of two-year-olds at church waiting to spend an hour with you.) It is children's disposition toward the world, their lack of concern for status and position, that Jesus is drawing attention to. Those who approach life with humility are great because God can freely work in them, displaying his power. Jesus' use of a child to teach the disciples serves as a rebuke to them for their pride.

The law is this: Unless you change and become like children, you cannot enter the kingdom of heaven. It's that simple and that profound. Jesus is prodding our transformation by telling us right at the beginning that humility is the first step toward a relationship with God.

His stern warning in verse 6 is not to be taken lightly. Jesus is using a strict comparison to make his point. It would be better for you to suffer a terrible drowning fate than to lead "little ones" (that is, humble people) astray. Better to go down drowning than to cause others to sin! Better to die a thousand deaths than to make others fall short of God's standard! Imagine a judgment that is worse than a terrible drowning. You get the idea.

Joining the Conversation (20 minutes). "God opposes the proud but gives grace to the humble," the Bible says (1 Peter 5:5). This is an interesting statement. It does not say that God withholds grace from the proud—rather, he opposes them. Yet we often try to work in opposition to God. Reminds me of that Broadway hit of years ago titled "Your Arm's Too Short to Box with God"!

The humility-factor evaluation is part fun, part probe. It is designed to help people begin looking at the real issue—their own pride.

In question 9, "little ones" is probably any believer or kingdom seeker. Jesus compares them to little children because they engage humbly, without much pretense. Kids wear their emotions on their sleeve, never hiding how they really feel (we learn to do that as adults). It is that unpretentious attitude that Jesus loves. And he hates to see such people led astray. He rebuked the Pharisees and teachers of the law for heaping burdens (extraneous laws and rituals) on people who seek the truth (Matthew 23:1-4) and threatened them with great judgment for doing so.

Sin is "missing God's mark," being off target and out of the will of God. To follow God requires faith, and "everything that does not come from faith is sin," according to Romans 14:23. So to intentionally cause others to miss God's way and to lead them astray is deplorable to Jesus. So awful is this that Jesus describes the judgment of the person who commits such a sin in very graphic terms.

Connecting Our Stories (20 minutes). God warns us in order to protect us. Here Jesus is protecting us from judgment and from the consequences of sin and rebellion against God. Sin is so offensive to God that Jesus paints a picture of self-mutilation as being preferable to sin: do whatever it takes to keep from sinning and from leading others into sin. For sin, as James says, "gives birth to death" (James 1:15). Spiritual, physical and emotional death is the result of turning away from God

Finding Our Way (10 minutes). The focus here is change—changed attitudes and hearts. How do we humble ourselves and seek God? What must we lay aside (see Hebrews 12:1) in order to invite the transforming work of God? Jesus has prodded us along by warning us and by giving us a beautiful picture of humility—a child.

Praying Together (10 minutes). Some of your prayer time can be devoted to personal evaluation and reflection. Ask the Spirit to root out any pride that exists and to create a humble heart in each member. If necessary, confess any wrongdoing within the group and pronounce forgiveness.

Consider This. Ask participants for any closing reflections. Review briefly how Jesus has been teaching us as he

- shatters our illusions
- renews our mind
- exposes our motives
- confronts our unbelief
- raises our hopes
- prods our transformation

Then be sure to take some time to celebrate the completion of this series of explorations. It has been challenging, presenting your group with some difficult words from Jesus, our Provocative Teacher. Yet you persisted and fruit was borne—so set aside some time to say, "Yea, God!"